Fifty Things
I Want My
Son to Know

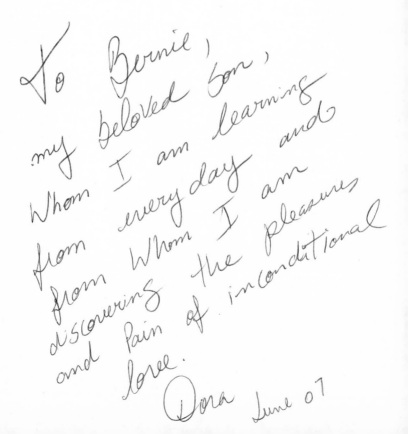

To Bernie,
my beloved son,
Whom I am learning
from everyday and
from Whom I am
discovering the pleasures
and pain of inconditional
love.
Dora June 07

Fifty Things
I Want My
Son to Know

Roger Rueff

ISBN: 0-7407-1462-7

Library of Congress Catalog Card Number: 00-106956

Book design and composition by Kelly & Company, Lee's Summit, Missouri

To Dylan Michael Rueff.
Enough said.

Introduction

If you were given the chance to write a guidebook on life for your child, to put together a small volume of important reminders gleaned from your own experience on Earth, how would you go about it? What would you say?

Those were the questions I found myself pondering awhile back when, in the midst of some difficult times, a small, clear voice inside me turned its attention toward my son, Dylan, who had recently turned six. What advice could I offer him concerning the matter of how to live—how to succeed in his goals and relationships and remain human while doing so?

This book is my answer.

Basically, it happened this way.

A few years ago I found myself embroiled in a number of coincident crises, including joblessness, a career change, and the beginnings of what proved to be a long and difficult divorce. One afternoon while I was out on an errand, a small, inspirational thought occurred to me in the form of a poetic proverb. It was nothing earth-shaking, just a brief, significant reminder to myself—

something to keep in mind as I struggled to hold things together from one day to the next. As a writer, I'm accustomed to paying attention to things like that, so I pulled into a gas station parking lot, stopped the car, and jotted down the proverb on some handy piece of scrap paper—probably a cash register receipt or a napkin from a fast-food restaurant.

The next day, something similar occurred. Another proverb came to mind and again I wrote it down. The following week it happened again—and again sometime after that. It was as though some deep, resonant voice inside me was trying to make itself heard, and my job was simply to let it. So I did.

Over the course of the next year or so, two things happened. One, I got used to thinking in terms of the proverbs—they provided a handy context for couching my observations about life. And, two, it gradually dawned on me that I wasn't recording the proverbs for myself, I was writing them for *Dylan*. The voice inside me was putting together a collection of things I wanted him to know and understand as he got older. It was piecing together a small, personal handbook on how to live.

It was answering the question, *What would you say?*

When the crises subsided, I returned to the collection of proverbs to see what I had. Some I threw out; others I kept and worked on—pruning, rephrasing, and rearranging until, at last, I arrived at what I considered to be a satisfying form of the collection. Fifty proverbs made the final cut—hence the title, which suggested itself early on: *Fifty Things I Want My Son to Know.*

So here it is. The book I wrote for Dylan—and for anyone else who, like me, can benefit from a gentle reminder now and then that things are not as dire as they seem, that we exist apart from the world we inhabit and can shed our attachment to the things that bring us grief if we try. That grief, too, has its purpose. That we can be virtuous, strong, wise, and happy—all the tools are inside us already; we have only to use them. That life is complex and simple all at once (not to mention an enigma sometimes). That what matters is here and now.

My hope is that Dylan will keep this book with him as he grows older. And that he'll return to it from time to time in the years ahead—for encouragement and support or simply out of curiosity, each time gleaning more from the proverbs and seeing them in the richer light that shines from experience. And who knows? When he's old enough, maybe something inside him will pose the same sort of question that spawned this book: *If I were to write a handbook for my children, what would I say?*

I can't wait to read his reply.

Fifty Things
I Want My
Son to Know

Thing One

That he is God.

That Divinity wakes when he opens his eyes,
    touches Itself with his fingers,
    inhales Itself with his lungs.

That through him, God admires all that is.

That the sidelong glance of the Godhead
falls upon him every hour
through the eyes of those
who, too, are God
    without knowing.

That to say he is not God
is to say that God does not exist in him,
is to say that God does not exist.
    Which is blasphemy.

Thing Two

That he must sow what he seeks to grow what he wants to find.

That life is a soil ready
to nourish the potent deed.
That all good seeds are sown for their own sake;
the harvest takes care of itself.

That if he wants love and affection,
    he must become its source
    for others.
That if he wants enlightenment,
    he must be willing to teach.
That if he wants wealth,
    he must learn not to hoard
    what Nature has given to him.

Thing Three

That each meeting is an exchange.

That everyone who crosses his path
bears a gift.
A bit of magic
   torn from the cloth of life.
One missing piece to the puzzle
   of how to live.

That inside the gift
hides a genie
who grants one wish.
That to lure it into the open,
he must beckon it with his own—
the genie that hides in the gift
   he offers in return.
The thoughtful word.
The willing ear.
The timely smile.

That the genies are
our unseen media of exchange.

Thing Four

That each of us is home to a thousand
genies.

___

That they nap inside us,
each awaiting its turn.

That to summon the genie groomed
for the circumstance at hand,
he must squeeze into the moment,
whisper its name,
rouse it,
    and invite it to play.

Thing Five

That it hurts to stretch a metaphor too far.

Thing Six

That he was born in the woods.

With an ax,
a compass,
a handful of nuts and berries.

That he can chop his way through the underbrush,
or follow the needle where it leads,
or open his palm
    and come to terms with the fauna.

Thing Seven

That inside him lives a great oracle.

Whose throne he may approach,
or not,
when he finds himself wanting
    to know.

Who knows what he seeks
before he seeks it.
    And why.

That it is deaf
to the angry voices that gather at the temple gates,
seeking its crucifixion.

That sometimes it will turn him away
for his own sake
and whisper in his ear
before he goes,
    "Come back when you know one more thing."

Thing Eight

That not everything is a lesson.

That inside him lives a pupil
forever jotting notes.
That sometimes he must put down the pen
to hear what's being said
or, better yet, the bell that rings
for recess.

Thing Nine

That Truth is a pretty girl.

On the far side of the room.
He may approach her by half every hour
    but never kiss.

Thing Ten

That the high road has no guardrails.

And a couple of really nasty hairpin turns.

Thing Eleven

That Life prefers beauty.

That the fittest survive,
    but only what is lovely moves Life forward.
That weeds endure by defense,
succeed by being tenacious
    and hard to kill.
That flowers last by luring what they need.

That some great thing wants them.
Otherwise, the world would be nothing but weeds.

Thing Twelve

That there are no weeds.

Or flowers.

Only plants.

Thing Thirteen

That doing and being weigh the same.

That everyone who is must do.
That all who do are.
That Nature purges those who are and do not
and those who do without being.
    One by starvation—
    the other by accident.

That doing makes it possible to be.
That being makes the doing worth the fuss.

That doing and being
are the handshake of greeting
for a man at peace with himself.

Thing Fourteen

That God is deaf.

That the soul shouts loud and long—
entreating God for favors,
decrying the injustices of fate,
pleading until it is hoarse
and even after.
    That God hears none of this.

That in the soul's most quiet corner,
something meek, with nimble fingers, stands
signing the true prayer.

That God is a lover of nuance.

Thing Fifteen

❧

That he exists outside the spotlight.

That those without fame live also.
That even when the camera stops rolling,
life goes on.

Thing Sixteen

That he need not fear what he wants.

That no wicked Other has planted his desires
like traps along the way
to who he is.
That he need not tiptoe
on the path
    to know himself.

That his heart is not a minefield.
That only what is dead desires not.

Thing Seventeen

That inside him is a marketplace.

Crowded with buyers and sellers,
the face of every one of which
is his.

That here sits a beggar,
there a prince
borne on pillows from his birth.
A girl selling flowers
picked this morning.
A man with rugs
he swears were sewn by hand.
A thief who waits in the alley
to steal his purse.

Thing Eighteen

❧❧

That his soul does not want to be found.

That he will not discover it
    but must never abandon the search.
That once or twice he will glimpse it
like a shadow
cast by a shooting star.
That each time he thinks he has found it,
grabbed it,
made it his at last—
he will find in his hands an echo.
Nothing more.
           Nothing more.
                  Nothing.
                        More.

That what he seeks will laugh at him
from across a great canyon.
That its footprints
and campfires—
the twigs it breaks in flight—
are all he will ever,
can ever,
know.

That it throws its voice.

Thing Nineteen

That the goal of the game is to play.

That conquest demands elation—
defeat, the deepest sense that all is lost.
That joy and sorrow feed both sides of the soul.

That a soul too full of either
will not fly.

Thing Twenty

❧❧

That he may, at any time, become the Adult.

That no barrier stands
between his heart and right action.
There is no rushing river to cross.

The Adult stands at the stove, fixing dinner,
or sits on the patio, reading—
a keen ear tuned to the cry for help,
the shriek of discovery,
the quiet tap on its shoulder
for a moment of its time.
That sometimes he must watch the hands
    stirring the pot
or listen
    as each page turns.

That if he dares to read over his shoulder,
he may be surprised
how many big words he knows.

Thing Twenty-one

❧

That the Child inside him is always up for a game.

That while he dashes from bow to stern,
setting the sails of life,
cursing the high seas,
and the calms—
the Child waits below,
reading a comic book,
shuffling a fresh deck of cards,
thinking up stories to tell.

That while he works on the house he was given,
mending the woodwork,
tending the garden,
grooming a showcase home—
the Child sits in a playground swing
two blocks away,
staring down at the sand,
making figure eights with its toes,
hoping the chores will end soon,
so he can come out and play.

Thing Twenty-two

❦❦

That sorry *does* do it.

Thing Twenty-three

That a flower is a pattern ongoing.

That what survives through the seasons
and years
is merely the flower idea.
Whispered from one generation to the next.
Passed on like a secret—
    the Fellowship of Flowers'
    sacred pact.

That all things living play out a code.
A sentence spoken under God's breath.
An aside in a language we barely understand—
    its grammar
    pure intent.

Thing Twenty-four

That darkness fears the tongue.

That despair thrives in silence—
grows toward it
    like a burgeoning shoot seeks the sun.
Drawing for its sustenance
    the unnamed fear,
    the unshared heartache,
             the anger held within.

That it basks in the rays
of something true unsaid.

Thing Twenty-five

That the only safe place is this moment.

That Guilt and Fear are ogres who feed on the soul—
    one mottled with ancient running sores,
    the other flecked with scars
        from wounds not yet made.
That this moment has no room for them;
he is always protected
    Now.

That this moment seems impossibly thin,
a safe house with paper walls,
    but opens to a greater world beyond.

That the greater world is larger
than all other worlds combined,
because it reveals itself wholly
all at once.

That the greater world of this moment
    possesses no borders;
it simply is.

Thing Twenty-six

❧ ❧

That he must become a man he can
trust.

Or spend his life
keeping very close watch
on himself.

Thing Twenty-seven

That God has buried a plan for his life inside him.

Surrounded it with chests
full of opulent treasure.
There is no map saying: "X marks the spot."
Only a tale passed down
by word of mouth.
That to find the riches, he must ask himself,
"If I were God, where would I hide such a thing?"
    "But wait! I am!
     I must have put it . . .

                                there."

Thing Twenty-eight

That he need not be the sheep nor the wolf.

Nor the shepherd
watching over his flock.

That he can be the poet lying
on the hill across the way
brewing some new potion
    made out of words.
Soothed by the bleating.
Amused by the stalker and the stalked.
Drunk with the thoughts of a girl
    and how nothing else matters.

Thing Twenty-nine

That the day may come when he looks down his nose at himself.

That the proper response involves his middle finger.

Thing Thirty

That inside him is a yardstick.

He stood it on end
and pulled himself upright
to walk.

Uses it now
to trace straight lines
and dream of swatting
the occasional inside curve.

Will one day show his children
where the numbers have worn off
     from use.
May rap them
when they stretch too far
in reaching for their own.
     And then repent.

Will use it as a walking stick
and, finally, a cane.
That it will be the first thing
swallowed up by the flames
of his pyre.

Thing Thirty-one

That the world is a phone booth.

Crammed with those eager
to fit in.
That if he turns his back on the hubbub
and follows the poles till they end,
he may find himself
　　on the other end of the line.

Thing Thirty-two

That he needs no one's approval.

Not even mine.

Thing Thirty-three

That he is not immune from tribulation.

That peril walks beside him, chatting—
kicking stones,
its hands in its pockets,
feeling for something there.
That he must learn to laugh at its jokes
but never to share his secrets
        or invite it home for a beer.

That someday he will have to run
as far and as fast as he can.
That trouble will stumble behind,
        hanging on to his scarf.

Thing Thirty-four

That good pitching beats good hitting.

And life rewards the man in control of his stuff.

Thing Thirty-five

❧❧

That opinions are to talent what pocket change is to wealth.

Easy to carry around and show friends
but wanting
    when it comes to the important exchange.

Thing Thirty-six

That God is an echo.

That God may be found in that canyon
or cave
where the penitent go
to beckon themselves
alone.

Give me wisdom!

                    Be wise.

Give me peace!

                    Stop striving.

Bring love to me!

                    Love.

The voice to trust is that which never speaks.

Thing Thirty-seven

❧❧

That before him hangs a thick, black veil.

He holds it aloft,
gripped in his fists,
braced to keep the light
from hurting his eyes.

That someday his arms will grow weak
or stiffen
and, at the end, collapse
to let him see
the him that lives forever
staring back
    with a playful grin.

Thing Thirty-eight

❧☙

That his mind is a party.

Teeming with chattering guests.
That he cannot hide in the kitchen,
hoping they'll leave.
That when he most yearns for silence,
they will turn up the volume
     a notch.
That they'll offer jokes and compliments,
     adoration,
     consolation—
     anything for his ear.

That they'll worry him with their stories
even as he shows them the door,
and stand on the porch singing bawdy songs
     while he dreams.

Thing Thirty-nine

❧❧

That the island he lives on is shrinking.

And has been
from the moment he was born.

That, one day, he will find himself surrounded
on the beach—
the waves pressing in from all sides.
    That it will be his day
    to go to sea.

That how he fares from that moment on
will depend upon the temper of his boat.

That I cannot build the boat for him;
I can only hand him the hammer,
a saw,
and a rough sketch
of my own.

Thing Forty

❧

That the fighting will never stop.

That we are all like little children
on a long trip in the car—
beating each other up in the backseat
and every once in a while asking,
    "Are we there yet?"

Thing Forty-one

That he is what he is——not what he does.

The do-er who denies his task to seek a state of mind,
the be-er who forsakes his heart to do . . .
commit the same sin.

Thing Forty-two

That he is what he does—not what he is.

___

That karmic law pays no attention to titles.

Thing Forty-three

That regret is a pair of kid sisters.

Who follow him always,
tugging at his sleeves.

That one keeps a journal,
jotting what he could have done
and did not.
The other talks of a pleasant life
he might someday live
but won't.

That to save himself
from the nagging,
he must lead them to the center of the bridge
this moment is
and leap from the edge.

Thing Forty-four

That he lives alone.

That something stands
in the room where he dwells—
　　one hand on the cord
　　that opens and closes the blinds.
Observing the kids
on the other side of the courtyard,
　　who stand behind their own blinds
　　looking out.

That each of the windows
is made
　　of unbreakable glass.

Thing Forty-five

That the past and the future are phantoms.

That Was and Will Be are restless ghosts,
wandering the halls of a mansion—
    rattling chains,
    calling out in the night,
    haunting us all as we sleep.

Who obscure but never intrigue,
unsettle but never upset—
couching every mystery
in doubt.

That to send them away
he must rise from the bed
    and be forever waking from the dream.

Thing Forty-eight

That the Song of Life is a victory dance.

Because Death wins all the battles
but never the war.

Thing Forty-nine

That good religion hangs its hat on Nothing.

Its disciples kneel
only to offer a hand to someone fallen.
Never tithe
or hoard.

That their God plays hide-and-seek with them
to help them learn how to find.
And weeps for those
whom doctrine
puts to the leash.

That their liturgy reads only "Thank you."
Their only hymn—
an idle tune unsung.

That their names are not written in the Book of Life,
except in the dedication.
That they are eternal
as only the unnamed can be.
That every step of life
is their procession.

And since they worship everywhere,
their temple cannot be destroyed.

Thing Fifty

❧❧❧

That my love for him is beyond words.